God Is Creator & Redeemer

> Forever, O LORD, Your word is settled in heaven. Your faithfulness endures to all generations; You established the earth, and it abides.—Psalm 119:89–90

GOD'S WORD FOR ALL GENERATIONS

Answers
BIBLE CURRICULUM

Answers Bible Curriculum

Year 1 • Quarter 2 • Adult Student

Copyright © 2012 Answers in Genesis.

Printed in China.

Contents

Introduction 5

1 Creation: God Creates the World 7
   Prepare to Learn 8
   Studying God's Word 11
   The Order Matters 11
   God's Word in the Real World 12
   Prayer Requests 12

2 Creation Days 1–4 13
   Prepare to Learn 14
   Studying God's Word 17
   "What Is a Day?" video notes 17
   Days of Creation 18
   God's Word in the Real World 18
   Prayer Requests 20

3 Creation Days 5–6 21
   Prepare to Learn 22
   Days of Creation 25
   Studying God's Word 25
   Kinds of Critters 25
   God's Word in the Real World 26
   Prayer Requests 26

4 Dinosaurs and Dragons 27
   Prepare to Learn 28
   Studying God's Word 31
   "Dinosaurs and Dragon Legends" video notes 31
   God's Word in the Real World 32
   Prayer Requests 32

5 God Creates Adam and Eve 33
   Prepare to Learn 34
   Studying God's Word 38
   Two Creation Accounts? 39
   God's Word in the Real World 40
   Prayer Requests 42

6 How Old Is the Earth? 43
   Prepare to Learn 44
   Studying God's Word 47
   Calculating Earth's Age 48
   God's Word in the Real World 48
   Prayer Requests 50

7   Stewards of God's Creation **51**

Prepare to Learn 52

Studying God's Word 55

"Dominion" video notes 55

Stewards of God's Creation 55

God's Word in the Real World 56

Prayer Requests 56

8   Creation Compromise **57**

Prepare to Learn 58

Studying God's Word 61

Christian Views on Creation 61

"What's Wrong with Progressive Creation?" video notes 61

God's Word in the Real World 62

Prayer Requests 64

9   Corruption: Sin Enters the World **65**

Prepare to Learn 66

Studying God's Word 69

The Plan 70

God's Word in the Real World 71

Prayer Requests 72

10 Effects of the Fall **73**

Prepare to Learn 74

Studying God's Word 77

A Cursed Creation 77

"Was there Death Before Adam Sinned?" video notes 78

God's Word in the Real World 79

Prayer Requests 80

11 Cain and Abel **81**

Prepare to Learn 82

Studying God's Word 85

An Acceptable Sacrifice 85

God's Word in the Real World 86

Prayer Requests 88

12 The Hearts of Man **89**

Prepare to Learn 90

Studying God's Word 93

Pop Culture vs. Scripture 94

God's Word in the Real World 95

Prayer Requests 96

Introduction

The creation vs. evolution and young-earth vs. old-earth wars were being fought even before Darwin popularized the theory of evolution in the late 1800s. And today in the church, the battle continues.

Over the next 13 weeks we will be looking at what the Bible says about creation and the Fall. Can we trust God's Word when He tells us that He created everything in six days? Were those days long ages or normal-length days? Is Genesis 1–2 written as a historical account or an allegory? Did God simply use language that shepherds thousands of years ago could understand or did He give us a true account of the creation of everything? Can we fit evolution into the Bible? Should we try?

These are the kinds of questions we will be answering this quarter as we look at the text of the Bible as well as the findings of science. As we saw last quarter, God's Word is true, and we must never elevate man's word above God's Word.

We encourage you to read the Prepare to Learn section before class each week. This will provide important background information so that you will get more from each lesson.

For more information and links to online articles and videos, be sure to visit the Online Resource Page at www.AnswersBibleCurriculum.com.

Creation: God Creates the World

Key Passages

- Genesis 1:1–2:3; Jeremiah 23:24, 33:25; Psalm 69:34; Nehemiah 9:6

What You Will Learn

- How God's omnipotence is demonstrated in the creation account.

- How the biblical account of creation compares with the evolutionary model of the origin of the universe and life on earth.

Lesson Overview

The account of God's creation—by the Word of His mouth—reveals that He is the all-powerful, omnipotent Creator. The evolution model of creation conflicts dramatically with the biblical creation account of Genesis 1. We must rely on God's Word alone for the truth.

Memory Verse

Exodus 20:11

For in six days the Lord made the heavens and the earth, the sea, and all that is in them, and rested the seventh day. Therefore the Lord blessed the Sabbath day and hallowed it.

Prepare to Learn

SCRIPTURAL BACKGROUND

What scriptural background can we possibly give here? Before Genesis nothing but God in eternity past existed. Genesis 1 is the beginning of the universe, time, space, history, and all of life as we know it. In addition, Genesis is foundational to the rest of Scripture. It sets the tone for God's eternal plan of redemption.

From the very first verse, Scripture assumes God's existence without trying to prove it in any way. We must avoid using arguments that attempt to prove God by demanding evidence in the natural world. Man's need to prove God implies his intention to elevate his own autonomous reason above God's Word.

Though obviously presented with very little "background," the information given to us in the early chapters of Genesis is foundational to many important doctrines. Included in these are the Trinity (Genesis 1:26), death (Genesis 2:17), marriage (Genesis 2:24), sin (Genesis 3:6), the gospel (Genesis 3:15), and clothing (Genesis 3:21). The book of Genesis is to be taken as literal history provided by God to give us a glimpse of His majesty, wonder, creativity, and eternal purpose.

APOLOGETICS BACKGROUND

"In the beginning God created the heavens and the earth." This first verse in the Bible answers many questions for us, such as "Where did everything come from?" "Is there a God?" "When did time begin?" These are questions Christians often have trouble answering—not because they lack faith, but because they don't realize that answers to questions like these can be found in Scripture when it is examined closely.

When did time begin? Time itself began when God began to create the universe. He created time for man, but He Himself is not bound by time. He is eternal—the Alpha and the Omega—the beginning and the end (Revelation 1:8). God confirms this concept when He tells us that to Him a day is like a thousand years and a thousand years is like a day (2 Peter 3:8).

There are many opposing views of the Genesis account of creation that manipulate God's Word to include millions of years (the old-earth view). Many will try to persuade us that the creation account must be "proven" before being believed. Realistically, however, no account of origins can be proven—it must be accepted by faith. Christians must stand firm on biblical authority—God told us in His Word what happened and how He created: "By faith we understand that the worlds [universe] were framed [created] by the word of God, so that the things which are seen were not made of things which are visible" (Hebrews 11:3).

Does the order of creation matter? God specifically and systematically presents the order of His creation over a six-day period—so, yes, it does matter. The creation and evolution positions are in direct opposition to each other. Creationists believe God's Word as recorded.

Evolutionists believe in millions of years of slow change, from non-life to simple cells, to more complex plants and animals, and eventually to the organisms that exist today, including man. Those who embrace this position must reject God's Word because evolution does not harmonize with God's account of creation. Here are a few examples of the more obvious differences:

Evolutionary Ideas—Not True	Creation in Genesis—True	Reference
Sun before earth	Earth (Day 1) before sun (Day 4)	Genesis 1:1
Sun before light on earth	Light (Day 1) before sun (Day 4)	Genesis 1:3
Earth at same time as planets	Earth (Day 1) before other planets (Day 4)	Genesis 1:1, 1:14–15
Sea creatures before land plants	Land plants (Day 3) before sea creatures (Day 5)	Genesis 1:12–13, 1:20–23
Reptiles before birds	Birds (Day 5) before reptiles (Day 6)	Genesis 1:20, 1:23–24, 1:31
Creation took billions of years	God created in six normal 24-hour days.	Genesis 2:1–2

HISTORICAL BACKGROUND

Over the past 200 years, many scientists have developed unbiblical ideas and taught that the earth formed around 4.5 billion years ago. Unfortunately, many Christians have attempted to merge these long ages of geological time into the Bible's account of creation. A few of these views are:

1. The day-age view: a compromise belief that the days of Genesis 1 are actually vast ages of different lengths; based on secular dating methods.

2. The gap theory: a compromise belief that a vast period of time exists between Genesis 1:1 and 1:2 into which the geologic eras can be fit.

3. The framework hypothesis: a compromise belief that Genesis 1 is written in a non-literal, non-chronological way; based on secular dating methods.

4. Theistic evolution: a compromise belief that suggests God used evolutionary processes to create the universe and life on earth over billions of years.

5. Progressive creation: a compromise belief accepting that God has created organisms in a progressive manner over billions of years to accommodate secular dating methods.

These are all theories that attempt to fit evolution and/or millions of years into the Bible rather than taking God's Word for what it says.

Many Christians feel that the age of the earth is an unimportant side issue and that discussing it detracts from the gospel message. However, Christians must understand that *all* of Scripture is foundational to our faith. If we can set aside a literal six-day creation because it is considered "unscientific" or unpopular, then at what point do we determine the rest of the Bible to be true? Can we teach a virgin birth or a literal Resurrection? When we read the genealogy of Christ, which goes back to Adam, can it be taken literally? Believing the historical account of Genesis 1–11 is foundational to believing the rest of the Bible, and essential for understanding the gospel message.

For more information on this topic, go to the Online Resource Page.

Studying God's Word

Can evolution fit into the biblical account of creation?

Take notes as you study the following passages.

Genesis 1

Jeremiah 23:24

Jeremiah 33:25

Psalm 69:34

Nehemiah 9:6

The Order Matters

Working in small groups, complete The Order Matters worksheet.

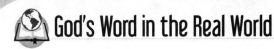 God's Word in the Real World

1. Many people claim that the Bible doesn't tell us how God created; it just tells us that He did create. Is this an accurate statement based on the text of Genesis 1?

2. As we approach the topic of creation vs. evolution in conversations with fellow believers, what should be our attitude?

3. Should our approach to supporting the biblical view of the Creation Week look different from discussing it with those who are not Christians? Why or why not?

4. If we suggest that the account of creation in Genesis is a myth or an allegory, what other doctrines would become mythical or allegorical—what doctrines find their basis in the first few chapters of Genesis?

5. How can understanding that God created the entire universe in six days by simply speaking it into existence help you to trust Him?

 Prayer Requests

Creation Days 1–4

Key Passages

- Genesis 1:1–19; Exodus 20:11

What You Will Learn

- The meaning of the word "day" (*yom*) as used in Genesis 1.

- How the phrase "according to its kind" relates to the limits of biological change.

Lesson Overview

The Hebrew word *yom*, used in context, points to the days of creation being regular 24-hour days. They will also explore creation Days 1–4 and be introduced to the idea of *kinds*.

Memory Verse

Exodus 20:11

For in six days the Lord made the heavens and the earth, the sea, and all that is in them, and rested the seventh day. Therefore the Lord blessed the Sabbath day and hallowed it.

SCRIPTURAL BACKGROUND

Through the book of Genesis, God intended for us to know specifically what He created and how long it took Him to create. The creation account allows us just a small glimpse of the power—the omnipotence—of our mighty God as He speaks, by the power of His Word, the entire universe into existence. Our lesson this week will include Days 1–4 (Genesis 1:1–19).

Day One includes the heavens, the formless earth, the waters covering the earth, and light which was separated from darkness. In addition to that, time itself began on the first day (Genesis 1:3–5).

On Day Two God created the "firmament" or "expanse." The Hebrew word is *raquiya*, and it has the idea of something spread out. This firmament was called "heaven," and this is what God created to separate the waters below from the waters above (Genesis 1:6–8).

God caused the dry land to appear and gathered the seas together to one place on the earth. He then spoke the grass, herbs, and trees into existence. This was Day Three (Genesis 1:9–13).

God again spoke and created lights in the expanse of the heavens—the sun, moon, stars, and other heavenly bodies appeared on Day Four (Genesis 1:14–19).

The Hebrew word for "created" is a word that depicts the making of something from nothing. God created our world *ex nihilo*—out of nothing that had previously existed (see Hebrews 11:3). The Bible reiterates that God is Creator in several other passages: Psalm 148:4–6; Isaiah 40:25–26; Colossians 1:15–16; Revelation 4:11. He spoke and it came to be. This is impossible for us to comprehend. But it should leave us breathless in the knowledge that He alone is worthy of our praise.

APOLOGETICS BACKGROUND

Those who want to fit evolution (and its millions of years) into the creation account in Genesis often reinterpret the 24-hour days in Genesis to be millions of years in length. As Christians who stand firmly on the authority of God's Word, we believe that a day is a day—24 hours—just as the Bible says.

We can understand the length of the days of creation by exploring the Hebrew word for "day" in Genesis 1, which is *yom* (rhymes with home). First, almost any word can have more than one meaning, depending on context. *Yom* can have several meanings. It can mean a day (an ordinary 24-hour day), the daylight portion of an ordinary 24-hour day (i.e., day as distinct from night), or an indefinite period of time describing an era (e.g., in the day of the judges, in the day of the Lord, or in my grandfather's day).

When determining the meaning of the word *yom* in the context of Scripture, theologians have relied on Hebrew dictionaries like the *Brown-Driver-Briggs Hebrew Lexicon*. This respected Hebrew resource actually gives Genesis 1 as an example of an instance in Scripture where the word *yom* refers specifically to a 24-hour day.

We also know that the Hebrew word *yom* always refers to an ordinary day when associated with a number and the words "evening" or "morning." In fact, whenever the word *yom* is used in the Old Testament in this way, it clearly refers to a 24-hour day. This simple study of the Hebrew language confirms the Genesis account of creation in six 24-hour days.

The study of Genesis and its accuracy as to the age of the earth is never far from a discussion of fossils. Fossils are the remains, traces, or imprints of dead plants or animals that have been preserved in the earth's near-surface rock layers. Secular scientists view fossils as evidence for a long prehistory for the earth and life on it—spanning millions of years.

Creationists view the same fossil deposits around the world and understand that these had to be formed by the rapid burial of countless billions of plants and animals. This rapid burial, when looked at through the lens of Scripture, is consistent with a global, catastrophic, year-long Genesis Flood which occurred, according to the biblical time frame, about 4,300 years ago.

Why is this an important issue? Because millions of years of history create an insurmountable problem regarding the gospel. The fossil record consists of the death of billions of creatures. It is a record of death, disease, suffering, cruelty, and brutality. The Bible makes it clear that God's creation was "very good" (Genesis 1:31) and that it was the sin of Adam that brought death, disease, and suffering into the world (Genesis 2:17; Romans 5:12). Death is the penalty for sin; Jesus Christ is the remedy. When Christians allow for death, suffering, and disease before sin, they are ignoring the exclusive message of the Cross and Christ's atoning work there, and they impugn the character of God who called His creation "very good."

HISTORICAL BACKGROUND

Prior to the 1700s, few believed in an old earth. Most people accepted the biblical account of Genesis and believed that the earth was approximately 6,000 years old. The subjective concepts of old age and uniformitarian geology—the view that slow and gradual processes, rather than a global catastrophe, created the earth's rock layers—started in the mid-1700s and 1800s. This was the beginning of the surrender of the truth of Genesis and the belief in millions of years of earth's history.

These concepts have weakened the culture of the western world and have affected the church because they attack the veracity of the very Word of God. Genesis 1 tells us exactly how God created the universe and exactly how long it took Him. To deny the very beginning verses of God's Word is to open the door of compromise to many other scriptural truths. The church is rushing down that road of compromise and must realize the urgent need to ignite a new reformation—calling believers back to the absolute authority of the Bible.

For more information on this topic, see the Online Resource Page.

Studying God's Word

Why is context such an important thing to understand when reading Scripture?

"What Is a Day?" video notes

Take notes as you view the "What Is a Day?" video.

Genesis 1

Genesis 2:4

Exodus 20:8–11

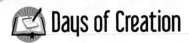 Days of Creation

Begin filling out the Days of Creation worksheet.

Take notes as you study the following passage.

Genesis 1:1–19

 God's Word in the Real World

1. What objections might you hear from others (or that you may have yourself) regarding the days in Genesis 1 being normal 24-hour days?

2. Peter 3:15 calls Christians to give an answer for their faith, but it also tells us that we should do it with meekness and fear, not with arrogance. Why is this important when considering an issue like the origin of the creation?

3. Some people suggest that the days of Genesis 1 could not be actual days since there wasn't even a sun to provide light for the earth—there can't be day and night or evening and morning without a sun. How could you use the text of Genesis 1 to explain this apparent problem?

4. What is the danger of suggesting that the days in Genesis 1 should be interpreted as long ages or as a myth that contains truth?

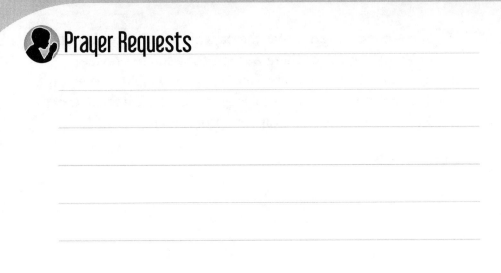

Prayer Requests

Creation Days 5–6

3

Key Passages

- Genesis 1:20–31; Leviticus 11:13–19

What You Will Learn

- What was created on Days Five and Six of Creation Week.

- The basic created kinds of Days Five and Six.

- The qualities of man that set him apart from the animals.

Lesson Overview

On Days Five and Six of Creation Week, God created flying animals, sea creatures, and land animals. God created these animals "according to their kinds." Man was created in God's image—unlike the animals. Because of this, God has provided a way for us to have a relationship with Him.

Memory Verse

Exodus 20:11

For in six days the Lord made the heavens and the earth, the sea, and all that is in them, and rested the seventh day. Therefore the Lord blessed the Sabbath day and hallowed it.

SCRIPTURAL BACKGROUND

"Then God saw everything that He had made, and indeed it was very good. So the evening and the morning were the sixth day" (Genesis 1:31). As we come to the end of Creation Week, God looked at His creation—and acknowledged it as very good. God provided us very specific information in this account—and we need to take notice of all He said.

So, let's take a closer look at the text and see the details God intended for us to grasp. "Let the waters abound with an abundance of living creatures, and let birds fly above the earth . . . . God created great sea creatures and every living thing that moves . . . according to their kind, and every winged bird according to its kind. . . . the living creature according to its kind: cattle and creeping thing and beast of the earth, each according to its kind . . . . the beast of the earth according to its kind, cattle according to its kind, and everything that creeps on the earth according to its kind" (Genesis 1:20–25).

When God repeats something, He expects us to listen. In the creation account God repeats 10 times that the living things He created were created according to their kinds. Here we see the Word of God plainly and simply providing the truth about creation. There is no room for man's idea of evolution. There is no way that all forms of life share a common ancestor because God's Word flatly denies that possibility.

As His final act of creation, God created man—in His image—to have dominion over all the animals and over all the earth (Genesis 1:26–27). Again, note that this account of creation challenges the very core of evolution. And that challenge is presented by the holy, omnipotent, omniscient God—we dare not deny His truth.

What does it mean that man is created in God's image? We are completely different from anything else created during the Creation Week. We have the capability to reason, to create, to intelligently communicate, and most importantly, to have a saving relationship—through our Lord and Savior Jesus Christ (John 3:16)—with the very God who created us. No animal could ever do that! Rejoice and celebrate our amazing God this week.

APOLOGETICS BACKGROUND

Our culture today is immersed in the idea of evolution. From TV, Hollywood movies, museums, billboards, cereal boxes, children's books, curriculum textbooks, even in our churches and Christian schools, the idea of life evolving from lower forms is taught as a better alternative than creation. We need to be diligent to teach that this is not true. God created all things according to their kinds to reproduce according to their kinds (see Scriptural Background above).

So all of this may lead us to the often asked question—what is a kind? The created kinds can be most closely described as *families* of animals. Each *family* is totally different from any other family. But let's go to God's Word for our answer. We've seen that the Bible's first use of the word "kind" is found in Genesis 1 when God created plants and animals according to their kinds. God used the term again when He instructed Noah to take two of every kind of animal onto the Ark (Genesis 6:20). After the Flood, God commanded that Noah bring out every living thing on the Ark (all the kinds) so that they could multiply on the earth (Genesis 8:17). By reading and comparing the language in these texts, it is clear that God intended all He created to reproduce within the boundaries of their created kinds—or families (Genesis 8:19).

Since the beginning of earth's history, there have been many different kinds (families) of animals. They are each distinct from one another. An animal or plant from one family has never turned into an animal or plant from another family.

That brings us right back to man's idea of evolution—it cannot be true. There has never been evidence of one kind of animal ever changing into a completely different kind of animal. We know that God's Word is and always will be our final authority. But in this case what we have observed from the beginning and still observe today confirms the truth of the Bible and exposes the lie of evolution.

HISTORICAL BACKGROUND

From the early days of the church, the Genesis account of creation was taken as a literal account of the creation of everything in six days about 6,000 years ago. It was only in the 18th century that some men began to cast doubt on the biblical time frame of creation and began to discuss millions of years of earth history. It was then that the idea of uniformitarianism was developed. This idea holds that present geological processes are the key to understanding the past. For example, secular geologists contend that because canyons today erode at slow rates by rivers cutting through them, they must have eroded just as slowly in the past. While there were a few in the church who held onto the Bible as authoritative, many influential clergy and scientists adopted this idea of uniformitarianism and the millions of years of earth history that accompanied it.

But how would that affect the biblical view of creation? Many scientists and even clergy needed to fit these supposed millions of years of earth history into the biblical account. From this attempt came such views as the day-age theory and the gap theory. The belief that the earth was millions of years old paved the way for the evolutionary ideas of Charles Darwin in the late 1800s. Evolution fit nicely into the idea of millions of years and further discounted God's holy Word.

As society and many in the church adopted these unbiblical ideas, doubt in God's Word as a true history of the world increased. Evolutionary ideas led to the belief that man was just an animal—more highly evolved, for sure—but still just an animal. This view has led to such social atrocities as abortion, slavery, euthanasia, and genocide. If man is just an animal, then why not kill him the way one would squash a mosquito?

But God's Word tells us we are created in God's image (Genesis 1:26). We are not animals. In fact we have been given dominion over the animals and the earth (Genesis 1:28). This knowledge should promote value and respect among humans. Only as hearts are changed by the gospel, and Scripture becomes the final authority, will we begin to see social injustice diminish.

For more information on this topic, see the Online Resource Page.

 **Days of Creation**

Complete the Days of Creation worksheet.

 **Studying God's Word**

What makes man distinct from the animals?

Take notes as you study the following passages.

Genesis 1:20–31

Leviticus 11:13–19

 Kinds of Critters

After viewing the "Kinds" video, complete the Kinds of Critters worksheet.

God's Word in the Real World

1. How would you explain to someone that the idea that man is just a highly evolved ape is absolutely incompatible with the Bible?

2. What social implications does an evolutionary view of mankind have?

3. How could you use Scripture to sit down with someone who does not believe there is a conflict in the biblical and evolutionary accounts of the origin of life and show them the conflicts?

4. How does knowing that Jesus is both the Creator and the Savior of the world help you to love Him more?

 # Prayer Requests

4
Dinosaurs and Dragons

Key Passages

* Job 40:15–24, 41:1–34

What You Will Learn

* The identity of the two dinosaur-like creatures described in the book of Job.

* The support, biblical and other, for man living alongside dinosaurs.

Lesson Overview

Dinosaurs were created on Day Six along with the other land animals, and lived with man. The book of Job mentions behemoth and leviathan—both dinosaur-like creatures. As we look through the lens of the Bible, the world of dinosaurs makes sense!

Memory Verse

Exodus 20:11

For in six days the Lord made the heavens and the earth, the sea, and all that is in them, and rested the seventh day. Therefore the Lord blessed the Sabbath day and hallowed it.

SCRIPTURAL BACKGROUND

We know that dinosaurs are perhaps used more than anything else to indoctrinate all of us into believing in millions of years of earth history. As we continue to explore Creation Week and the one who spoke all things into existence, we're going to take a more in-depth look at this very controversial subject—dinosaurs and dragons.

Let's begin in Genesis 1:1, "In the beginning God created the heavens and the earth." This was the beginning of time as we know it. Before this moment in history, nothing existed except God. And then God created the universe in six days, about 6,000 years ago!

As we move on to Day Six of the Creation Week, we learn that God created all the beasts of the earth, everything that creeps on the earth, and man (Genesis 1:24–27). This reveals some very critical information. We know dinosaurs are land animals; we know land animals were created on Day Six; we know man was created on Day Six; so man and dinosaurs lived together at the same time only 6,000 years ago!

God references dinosaurs again in the book of Job. As God is describing His greatness to Job, He reminds Job of the largest animal He created—the behemoth (Job 40:15–24). The biblical description of this animal does not fit any living animal we know of today. It does, in fact, fit the description of a dinosaur—a sauropod—one of the largest dinosaurs, created by God on Day Six.

And to give us even more confirmation, God describes the leviathan in the next chapter (Job 41:1–34). What an amazing creature that must have been! This creature is mentioned four other times in Scripture (Job 3:8; Psalms 74:14, 104:26; Isaiah 27:1). It is believed that this was some sort of mighty dinosaur-like sea monster able to overwhelm the hunter (Job 41:9), but not too fierce for God. And what about the burning lights that flash from his mouth and shoot out fire (Job 41:18–21)? This is a creature unheard of today yet repeatedly mentioned by God and may very well have been a fire-breathing creature.

As you prepare for this lesson, proceed confidently knowing that the entirety of God's Word is truth (Psalm 119:160) and it should always be our starting point and foundation when addressing questions presented by the world.

APOLOGETICS BACKGROUND

We mentioned above that dinosaurs and man were created on the same day of Creation Week—about 6,000 years ago. But is that what we hear around us? Absolutely not! "Dinosaurs died out millions of years ago and could never have lived with man!" Over and over this message is repeated with no regard to what God's Word says. Our response to this ultimately comes down to whether we trust God's Word or man's word. There can be no compromise. Where does your allegiance lie? What is your worldview?

Why is this important? The belief that dinosaurs lived and died millions of years before man attacks the very foundation not only of the Bible, but of the gospel. The Bible makes it clear that God's original creation was "very good" (Genesis 1:31). Yet the fossils of dinosaurs reflect death, disease, suffering, cruelty, and brutality. If we accept that these fossils represent millions of years of earth history, then we are accepting death in the world before Adam's sin.

The Bible tells us there was no death in the garden. Both animals and man were originally vegetarian (Genesis 1:29–30). It was Adam and Eve's sin against a holy God that brought judgment on the whole creation—death, both spiritual and physical (Genesis 2:17, 3:19). In fact, it was Adam's sin that provoked the first killing of an animal in God's very good creation—the animal (or animals) God killed to provide Adam and Eve with skins to cover their nakedness (Genesis 3:21).

This first shed blood in the Garden of Eden was a foreshadowing of the Savior—the Lamb of God who would take away the sins of the world (John 1:29). Jesus came to earth in order to provide payment for the consequence of sin—which is death—and to offer eternal life (Romans 6:23). So you see, when we accept the notion of millions of years of animal death before the creation and Fall of man, we contradict and destroy the Bible's teaching on death and the full redemptive work of Christ.

HISTORICAL BACKGROUND

Many believe the author of the book of Job was Job himself, who lived in the land of Uz (see Job 1:1). Most scholars agree that Job lived *after* the Flood of Noah's day (Job 22:16 makes an obvious reference to the global Flood). Based on the text, biblical researchers have determined that Job lived to be over 200 years old. His life span fits with the life spans of the early descendants of Noah recorded in Genesis 11. This is important to note because it reveals that Job (and other men) lived with dinosaurs (behemoth and leviathan) after the Flood.

There are also several extra-biblical accounts of dinosaurs living with man.

Legends from around the world tell of heroes who killed large, reptilian creatures. The ancient Europeans, for example, called these monsters dragons. They appear in art, literature, and folklore. There are many Native American legends as well—of flying reptiles.

Then we have petroglyphs—rock paintings of dinosaur-like creatures. Similar images have been found on old pottery.

Other known historical accounts and legends of dinosaurs and/or dragons include:

- A Sumerian story dating back to 2000 BC or earlier that tells of a hero named Gilgamesh, who, when he went to fell cedars in a remote forest, encountered a huge, vicious dragon. He slew it, cutting off its head as a trophy.

- When Alexander the Great (c. 330 BC) and his soldiers marched into India, they found that the local people worshiped huge hissing reptiles that they kept in caves.

- China is renowned for its dragon stories, and dragons are prominent on Chinese pottery, embroidery, and carvings.

- Who can overlook the story of St. George, popular in England, which tells of the hero who slew the dragon that lived in a cave?

- In the 1500s, a European scientific book, *Historia Animalium*, listed several living animals that we would call dinosaurs.

- Ulysses Aldrovandus, a well-known naturalist in the sixteenth century, recorded an encounter on May 13, 1572 near Bologna, Italy between a peasant named Baptista and a dragon whose description fits that of the small dinosaur *Tanystropheus*. The peasant killed the dragon.

Keep in mind that none of the above references use the word "dinosaur." We wouldn't expect to find the word in certain Bibles like the Authorized Version that was published in 1611. That's because the term dinosaur wasn't coined until 1841, not long after the bones of these great creatures were unearthed and studied. Before that, they were called dragons. You may notice that the Hebrew word *tannyn* is translated as dragon a number of times in the Old Testament. If you look at a King James Version translation, you'll see the word is still used in several places (Nehemiah 2:13; Psalm 91:13; Isaiah 27:1; Ezekiel 29:3).

None of the evidence that dinosaur-like creatures lived with man is deemed valid by evolutionists. Why? Because their worldview is based on their own presuppositions—that dinosaurs lived millions of years ago. This prevents them from even considering the evidence, whether historical or biblical. Our worldview needs to begin with God's Word as we rely on it for the foundation of all we believe.

For more information on this topic, see the Online Resource Page.

Studying God's Word

Did man and dinosaurs live together?

Take notes as you study the following passages.

Job 40:15–24

Job 41:1–34

"Dinosaurs and Dragon Legends" video notes

Take notes as you view the "Dinosaurs and Dragon Legends" video.

God's Word in the Real World

1. What is the importance, in our world today, of having an explanation for the existence of dinosaurs on a young earth?

2. How can you help children and others understand this issue from a biblical perspective?

3. How can dinosaurs be used as an opportunity to share the gospel?

4. Christians know that they will face ridicule from those who reject the Bible as the authority when trying to understand issues like dinosaurs. How do we deal with such criticisms?

Prayer Requests

God Creates Adam and Eve

5

Key Passages

- Genesis 2:4–25; 1 Corinthians 11:7–9,
  15:47–48; 1 Timothy 2:13; Mark 10:1–9

What You Will Learn

- How the biblical view of the origin of man compares to the evolutionary view.

- The biblical view of marriage.

- The connection between the accounts of creation in Genesis 1 and 2.

Lesson Overview

Genesis chapter 2 gives a more detailed account of Day Six, specifically the creation of Adam and Eve. God created man directly from the dust of the earth, and woman from his side; this is not compatible with the evolutionary view of man's origin.

God's design for marriage is one man and one woman for life.

Memory Verse

Exodus 20:11

For in six days the Lord made the heavens and the earth, the sea, and all that is in them, and rested the seventh day. Therefore the Lord blessed the Sabbath day and hallowed it.

SCRIPTURAL BACKGROUND

Genesis 1:26 records the creation of the first living human—the crowning point and finishing touch of God's creation. Man, both male and female, were brought to life in the midst of all the good things God had created. Imagine the awesomeness and comfort in the beauty they saw. And Adam would soon know that God's intention was for him to have dominion over it all.

The creation of Adam and Eve was much different from anything else God created. We know that God commanded everything into existence, "Let there be light" (Genesis 1:3); "Let there be a firmament" (Genesis 1:6); "Let the dry land appear" (Genesis 1:9); "Let the earth bring forth grass" (Genesis 1:11); and so on. But Scripture tells us that man is unique. This part of God's creation was not commanded into existence as all the others were, but was lovingly overseen by the Triune God, "Let Us make man in Our image, according to Our likeness" (G e n -

esis 1:26). God's sovereign plan demanded that this part of His creation be comprised of soul and spirit—created in His image. This creature of God's would walk with Him, talk with Him, and one day be redeemed by Him.

As we move to Genesis 2, we are introduced to more of the history of the Creation Week: "This is the history of the heavens and the earth when they were created . . ." (Genesis 2:4). Claiming that the Bible cannot be trusted, many suggest that Genesis 2 contradicts Genesis 1. However, this is not a different creation account, but a detailed account of Day Six. God, in His mercy and grace, recorded details of the sixth day in Genesis 2. God recounts for us the specific circumstances surrounding the creation of Adam and Eve. We learn that He brought Adam from the dust of the ground and breathed life into him—

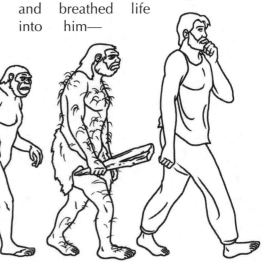

making him a living being (Genesis 2:7). God wisely decreed that man should not be alone (Genesis 2:18). This led to Adam naming the animals—the beasts of the field and the birds of the air (Genesis 2:19). After naming the various animals, it was clear there was no helper comparable to him (Genesis 2:20). But God had a solution. He formed Eve from Adam's side, bone of his bone and flesh of his flesh, to walk with him as a suitable, comparable helper (Genesis 2:21–23). Creating Eve for Adam, God instituted the sacred covenant of marriage, establishing that a man shall leave his father and mother and be joined to his wife so that the two shall become one flesh (Genesis 2:24). One man for one woman was God's plan for marriage from the beginning (Mark 10:6–9).

This exclusive revelation is provided for our edification from our Creator God, given to Moses through the inspiration of the Holy Spirit—that we would know Him and His omnipotence. What a privilege that He would share details that only He could know with us! But in order to appreciate the blessing of God's Word, we must have faith and believe it is our final authority—our only foundation and our starting point to discern truth from error. He tells us, "By faith we understand that the worlds were framed by the Word of God, so that the things which are seen were not made of things which are visible" (Hebrews 11:3).

APOLOGETICS BACKGROUND

We know that the truth of God's creation and the unique way He made Adam and Eve is in direct opposition to the idea of evolution. The image below is one used quite frequently to illustrate the "science" behind evolution—presenting as fact the story of human evolution from ape-like creatures over the past several million years. But we can't believe everything we see and despite its iconic status and widespread use, this image is not based on evidence, but on imagination. Actually there are very few fossil remains of men or apes (about 95 percent of the known fossils are marine invertebrates like clams, snails, squid, starfish, worms, corals, etc.)

In fact, many of the fossils of so-called human ancestors consist of little more than fragments of bone, yet they are touted by the science journals and media as "proof" of human evolution. Upon closer examination, all of these finds are either true apes or true humans—not something in between. The chart below presents alleged human relatives and how creation scientists might classify them:

Alleged Human Relative	Creationist Classification
Australopithecus afarensis (such as "Lucy")	extinct ape
Australopithecus africanus	extinct ape
Australopithecus boisei	extinct ape
Australopithecus robustus	extinct ape
Pan troglodytes and Pan paniscus (chimpanzee)	living ape
Gorilla gorilla and Gorilla beringei (gorilla)	living ape
Pongo pygmaeus and Pongo abelii (orangutan)	living ape
Ramapithecus	extinct ape (extinct orangutan)
Homo habilis	false category that mixes some human and some ape fossils
Homo floresiensis (the "hobbit")	human (dwarf, pygmy)
Homo ergaster	human
Homo erectus (e.g., "Peking man" and "Java man")	human
Homo neanderthalensis (Neanderthals)	human
Archaic Homo sapiens	human
Modern Homo sapiens	human

Our culture is flooded with evolutionary propaganda. However, when we begin with God's Word as our authority and determine to see the evidence through biblical glasses we will have no trouble recognizing the truth: we were directly created by God in His image to have a relationship with Him.

HISTORICAL BACKGROUND

The moral implications of the evolutionary view that man is merely an animal evolved from an ape are increasingly evident in our culture today. For example, many contend that because man is an ape, the ape-like or "primal" urges that we have for violence and sexuality can be excused because of our evolutionary history. Permeating every part of our culture, the idea of evolution has made many in our society calloused to social issues like abortion, racism, euthanasia, and genetic engineering. After all, if man is just an animal, a product of random, cosmic accidents, can an absolute moral code even exist? If an absolute moral code does exist, where did it come from? In an evolutionary society, morality is what the majority decides it to be or whatever makes you feel good. Consequently, each person determines his or her own idea of right and wrong. But this thinking is inconsistent and absolute morality cannot be the result of subjective personal choices. We can't all be right and all be wrong. This line of thinking promotes the "might makes right" attitude. The one with the most strength or power will eventually overcome the others in the struggle for survival.

As our society drifts further and further from the authority of God's Word, we will continue to see a decline in moral integrity.

If we discount the words of God in the very first book—Genesis—how can we stand on any of it? If we accept that man is an animal and not a created, living being made in the image of God, we won't consider Him worthy of our respect and love. On the other hand, as believers who preach the gospel and stand firmly on God's Word, boldly proclaiming it as our foundation for understanding right and wrong, we can affect a change in individuals that just may bring our society back to a Christian worldview.

For more information on this topic, see the Online Resource Page.

Studying God's Word

How does evolution undermine the doctrine of marriage?

Take notes as you study the following passages.

Genesis 2:4–25

1 Corinthians 11:7–9

1 Corinthians 15:47–48

1 Timothy 2:13

Mark 10:1–9

 Two Creation Accounts?

Skeptics of the authority of the Bible have suggested that the accounts of the Creation Week given in Genesis 1 and 2 contradict one another. Using the challenges below, develop responses to the skeptics using God's Word, especially Genesis 1 and 2, to support your explanations.

Challenge: Genesis 1 says that the land animals were created before mankind, but Genesis 2:19 says God formed the animals and brought them to Adam, who had already been created, and then formed Eve later. (Hint: the ESV, NIV, and Tyndale translate the passage "God had formed every beast.")

Challenge: Adam could not have named millions of species of animals in part of one day.

God's Word in the Real World

1. What forms of "marriage" do we see in society today, and what is the biblical error in those forms of relationships?

2. How do we respond to people we know who are living in relationships that are sinful (e.g., adultery, fornication, homosexuality)?

3. Many people, Christians included, seek to make an argument for biblical marriage based on statistics of "healthy and happy" families. Is this an adequate argument to make? Why or why not?

4. Genesis 1 and 2 make it perfectly clear that Adam and Eve were specially created by God, not evolved from animal precursors. How can you help Christians who believe in the evolution of mankind to see the error in that thinking?

5. Abortion and euthanasia are important topics in the world we live in. How does the truth from Genesis 1 and 2 help us to have an answer to how to deal with these situations?

6. If you ever hear from a skeptic that Genesis 1 and 2 contradict one another, how can you respond to that claim?

Prayer Requests

6

How Old Is the Earth?

Key Passages

- Genesis 5:1–32, 11:10–26;
  1 Chronicles 1:17–27; Luke 3:34–38

What You Will Learn

- Sources of the biblical and secular ages of the earth.

- The connection between the age of the earth and the authority of Scripture.

Lesson Overview

The Bible provides a clear date for creation, showing a young earth. The radiometric dating methods, which many use to determine the earth's age as billions of years old, are flawed and contradict the clear teaching of God's Word.

Memory Verse

Exodus 20:11

For in six days the Lord made the heavens and the earth, the sea, and all that is in them, and rested the seventh day. Therefore the Lord blessed the Sabbath day and hallowed it.

📖 Prepare to Learn

SCRIPTURAL BACKGROUND

Begin your preparation this week by reading Genesis 5 and Genesis 11:10–26.

So, now that you've read these genealogies, is your head spinning? We often rush through the genealogies of the Bible, laughing at our inability to pronounce the difficult names. But this time, take note of the details given in these two chapters. Genesis 5 recounts the ten generations before the Flood; Genesis 11 lists the ten generations after the Flood. When God includes such specific details, He intends for us to take notice.

Unlike a genealogy that simply lists the order of lineage, these passages contain ages and enough detail for the reader to determine the time span. They serve as "birth certificates," and allow us to calculate the time from Adam to Abraham. Each generation builds on the one before it, so we can add the years together to determine when Adam was created and the approximate age of the earth.

As we add up the years from Adam to Abraham, we get approximately 2,000 years. Historically it has been agreed upon by Christian and non-Christian historians alike that Abraham lived about 2,000 years before Christ. If we add the 2,000 years that have passed since Jesus's birth, we get an accurate age of roughly 6,000 years.

Were there billions of years that passed *before* Adam was created? No! The Bible says that Adam was created on the sixth day of creation (Genesis 1:26, 31) and that God created at the "beginning" (Genesis 1:1). Jesus Himself confirmed His belief in the creation account when He acknowledged that Adam and Eve were created at "the beginning of creation" (Mark 10:6).

There are many Christians and non-Christians who, in an attempt to make the universe older than it is, will say there are gaps in the genealogies recorded in Genesis. They argue that the word *begat* allows for generation skipping. However, the Hebrew word for begat (*yalad*) means a literal father/son relationship. Nowhere in the Old Testament is *yalad* used in any other way than to mean a single-generation (father/son or mother/daughter) relationship.

The genealogies are important to our history and should be read just as they are written. They are given to us to verify that the Bible is real history and that we are all descendants of a real man, Adam. We can trust these genealogies to give us accurate information because they are a part of the infallible, inerrant Word of God.

APOLOGETICS BACKGROUND

The belief that scientists have "proved" the earth to be billions of years old is a major reason many in the church have abandoned the biblical account of creation. However, contrary to popular belief, radiometric dating does not prove the earth is old.

All radiometric dating methods are based on the rate that radioactive elements decay in the rocks. Geologists refer to "parent" elements in rock decaying to "daughter" elements in the rock. By measuring how much "parent" and "daughter" elements are in a specimen, scientists try to calculate how old it is.

However, these methods are based on assumptions that are neither testable nor provable. These old-earth geologists come up with faulty dates because they are relying on faulty assumptions. These assumptions are:

1. The assumption that we know the starting conditions of these rocks—particularly the ratio of parent atoms to daughter atoms in the rocks to begin with. No one can definitively explain the starting conditions because no one was there when they were formed. It is impossible to know the ratio when the rock was formed, so secular scientists assume there was 100% parent and no daughter.

2. The assumption that all of the daughter atoms found in a rock were formed from the parent atoms in the same rock. We have no way of knowing for sure that all of the daughter atoms in a rock came from parent atoms in the same rock. Contamination of some sort, from ground water, for example, could add or eliminate parent and/or daughter atoms to the rock, making any dating of this type unreliable.

3. The assumption that the rate of decay has always been constant. This is a dangerous assumption given that we weren't there and we don't know if the rate of decay has been the same over thousands of years.

In addition to these assumptions, there are documented examples of inaccurate radiometric dating. Following are just a few examples:

- A sample of the lava dome in the Mount St. Helens crater (that had been observed to form and cool in 1984) was analyzed in 1996. It contained so much argon-40 (daughter atoms) that it had a calculated "age" of 350,000 years!

- Lava flows on the sides of Mt. Ngauruhoe, New Zealand, known to be less than 50 years old, yielded radiometric "ages" of up to 3.5 million years.

- The same basalt flows on the top of Grand Canyon were tested using three different dating methods. The "ages" calculated were 916 million years, 1.143 billion years, and 2.6 billion years!

God's Word unmistakably teaches a young earth and universe. God has ensured the accurate recording and preservation of His eyewitness account of the earth's history, which Jesus Christ endorsed repeatedly during His earthly ministry. We must have confidence in what God has revealed to us in His Word and not allow man's ideas to cause us to reinterpret it or compromise it in any way.

HISTORICAL BACKGROUND

For centuries Christians have believed that God created the world in six literal days roughly 4,000 years before Jesus's birth and that He judged the world by destroying it in the Flood of Noah's day. It is only over the last 250 years that questions about the Bible's record of time have arisen. Why? Christians and non-Christians swayed by the words of men began to try to fit billions of years of earth history into the Bible. The anti-biblical, philosophical assumptions that were used to interpret rocks and fossils threw the door wide open for doubting, manipulating, and questioning God's Word.

Even before the technology of radiometric dating was available, the shift in belief from the young earth to the faulty old-earth theories invented by man was leading to the idea of Darwinian evolution. Consequently, an avalanche of anti-biblical science appeared on the scene. It wasn't long before many church leaders began to embrace the old-age theories and made efforts to fit the ages into the Bible. Today, placing man's knowledge above what Scripture says has become commonplace. Sadly, interpretations of science, and tradition, often influence Christians more than Scripture itself.

But does the age of the earth really matter? Consider this. The Bible gives a detailed record of the age of the earth in the Genesis genealogy passages. Choosing to discount that part of the Bible because it doesn't line up with what we've heard from the scientific community, or the media, is placing man's knowledge above the authority of Scripture. If we are unable to take Genesis 1–11 as documented history, then how are we to believe the rest of the Bible? The Bible must be the final authority on all the matters it speaks of—not just the moral and spiritual. Every Word of God is true. It is the history book of the universe and we dare not presume to know more than the Creator God.

For more information on this topic, see the Online Resource Page.

# Studying God's Word

Does the age of the earth matter?

Take notes as you study the following passages.

Genesis 5:1–11

Genesis 11:10–26

1 Chronicles 1:17–27

Luke 3:34–38

_____

_____

_____

_____

Calculating Earth's Age

Complete the Calculating Earth's Age worksheet.

Genesis 5

_____

_____

_____

_____

God's Word in the Real World

1. In what areas of our culture do the questions about the age of the earth typically get asked?

2. As we think about the vast difference in the descriptions of the age of the earth—6,000 versus 4.5 billion—how is this debate primarily a debate about the authority of Scripture?

3. Should our goal in a conversation with an unbeliever over the age of the earth be to get them to agree that the earth is young?

4. How could you use the passages we have looked at today to help answer the questions of those who doubt the Bible's authority on the issue of the age of the earth?

Prayer Requests

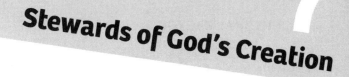

Stewards of God's Creation

7

Key Passages

- Genesis 1:26–31, 2:15, 2:19–20, 8:20–9:3

What You Will Learn

- The role of mankind in God's creation.
- God's faithfulness in sustaining His creation.

Lesson Overview

At creation God gave man the responsibility to provide good stewardship over His creation. But it is God who ultimately sustains and upholds all things by His power. We can turn to biblical principles in order to execute this God-given responsibility properly.

Memory Verse

Exodus 20:11

For in six days the Lord made the heavens and the earth, the sea, and all that is in them, and rested the seventh day. Therefore the Lord blessed the Sabbath day and hallowed it.

SCRIPTURAL BACKGROUND

Our God is the Creator and Sustainer of all the universe—everything we have comes from Him and it all belongs to Him. "In the beginning God created the heavens and the earth" (Genesis 1:1). "The sea is His, for He made it; and His hands formed the dry land" (Psalm 95:5). "The earth is the Lord's, and all its fullness" (Psalm 24:1). "For every beast of the forest is Mine, and the cattle on a thousand hills" (Psalm 50:10). "Your faithfulness endures to all generations; You established the earth, and it abides" (Psalm 119:90). God's creation clearly brings Him glory and He rejoices in His works (Psalm 104:31). We can rejoice, too, in God's graciousness to us each day as we appreciate the beauty and wonder around us. However, we must be diligent to respect it—because it does not belong to us.

When God created the world, it was perfect—it was all very good (Genesis 1:31). Man and all of creation lived together without any stress in a harmonious environment. But God did provide a hierarchy of authority. He intended that Adam and Eve be the ones to tend the garden and keep it (Genesis 2:15). He instructed them to multiply and fill the earth, and to have dominion over it and all of its creatures (Genesis 1:28). This "Dominion Mandate" ordained by God gives all of us, as the heirs of Adam, a special responsibility—to care for God's earth with diligence, concern, and from a biblical perspective.

What this means, however, is not always easily determined. Because of the high profile of this issue, you will come across many strong opinions. God did create resources for man's use in sustaining life. But we find today those who want to abuse the resources out of greed and selfishness, causing needless loss and destruction in other areas. We see also the overly enthusiastic conservationists who appear to worship the creation more than the Creator—clearly a position not ordained by God (Romans 1:25). What we need to remember is to consult the full counsel of God's Word in these matters. Because this is a sin-cursed world that is far, far from perfect, this may mean weighing each specific decision we make in this area based on the circumstances and expected results of that decision, while asking the question, "How does this line up with biblical principles?"

As you confront this issue, remember that Solomon in all his wisdom reminds us that there is a time to plant and a time to pluck what is planted, a time to kill and a time to heal, a time to break down and a time to build up, a time to keep and a time to throw away (Ecclesiastes 3:1–8).

Ultimately, this is an area that must be covered in prayer and balanced carefully between abuse to God's creation and environmental idolatry. It is God's creation. He made it and He will destroy it by the Word of His mouth at His appointed time (2 Peter 3:7). Meanwhile, He has promised to preserve it: "While the earth remains, seedtime and harvest, cold and heat, winter and summer, and day and night shall not cease" (Genesis 8:22).

APOLOGETICS BACKGROUND

The big issue surrounding the earth's environment today is global warming, or climate change. We are barraged with claims and facts being presented—leaving us more confused than ever. There appear to be five recurring claims. We'll take a quick look at those here.

Claim #1: Global warming is really happening. Yes, this is true. According to the National Climatic Data Center, the average global surface temperature has risen approximately 1.2°F (0.7°C) since 1880. We do not know exactly what has caused this warming.

Claim #2: Humans are causing global warming. Again, it seems to be true that addition of carbon dioxide to the atmosphere by man's activities has increased the global temperature. However, the CO_2 (carbon dioxide) in the atmosphere is not the sole cause of this warming. And it has been determined that the warmer climate itself can actually produce more CO_2—giving a distorted measure of the cause and effect of CO_2 in the atmosphere.

Claim #3: Global warming will cause the extinction of animals. First of all, many animals had gone extinct long before the issue of global warming was considered, and species continue to go extinct all the time. The woolly mammoth and the Miohippus (a small, three-toed woodland horse) are examples of animals found in the fossil record that are today extinct. Although there are predictions that many animals will become extinct by 2050 due to climate change, currently there are no documented extinctions resulting from global warming.

Claim #4: The oceans will rise dramatically in the next century. There is no hard scientific evidence currently available to back up this prediction.

Claim #5: Global warming will cause more weather catastrophes. Again, there is not sufficient evidence to make this claim. In fact, there are conflicting reports. Some blame global warming for the increase in hurricanes, tornadoes, floods, droughts, and extreme temperatures, while other studies have determined that global warming is not to blame.

From a biblical perspective, we know that we live in a world groaning from the effects of sin (Romans 8:22). The earth has been established by God and its future lies in His hands. Because of the credibility of God's Word, we can be sure that the earth will be purged by fire in the future (2 Peter 3:10–12)—not destroyed because of CO_2 emissions.

HISTORICAL BACKGROUND

In considering the history of global warming, we find that evidence does suggest that the created world was warmer than the world today. In fact, it wasn't until after the global Flood of Noah's day about 4,300 years ago—only about 1,700 years after creation—that conditions were right to form permanent ice, which prompted the earth's one and only Ice Age. Scientists believe that the Ice Age peaked around 500 years after the Flood.

As stated above, we know that the average global surface temperature has risen approximately 1.2°F since 1880. We also know that the changes in atmospheric carbon dioxide—the alleged cause of global warming—do not always correlate well with changes in the earth's temperature. For example, the temperature of the earth rose from 1910 to 1940 at a higher rate than the levels of carbon dioxide found in the atmosphere.

We also have indication that although the temperature of the earth has dropped since 2002, the carbon dioxide levels continue to rise. And it has been discovered that there were substantial changes in global temperatures in the ninth and seventeenth centuries, yet this could not have been a result of industry contaminating the air with CO_2.

Historically, there doesn't seem to be any conclusive pattern as to how the temperature of the earth reacts to those of us who live on it. We do know that the earth is God's and we are its caretakers. We have no idea how long the earth will last—but we are called to use biblical principles and judgment in maintaining it until Christ returns and it is renewed in the Consummation (Revelation 21:1).

For more information on this topic see the Online Resource Page.

 Studying God's Word

Can recycling become idolatry?

Take notes as you study the following passages.

Genesis 1:26–31

Genesis 2:15

Genesis 2:19–20

"Dominion" video notes

Take notes as you view the "Dominion" video.

Stewards of God's Creation

Complete the Stewards of God's Creation worksheet.

 God's Word in the Real World

1. How can we make the biblical case for using the earth's resources for our benefit?

2. What are the dangers of becoming too involved in environmental causes as a church?

3. As we encounter people who have genuine fears about the threats of global warming, how can we use Scripture to share the truth of the matter with them?

4. The media is constantly presenting messages that promote worship of the creation rather than the Creator. How do we guard ourselves against those false influences?

 Prayer Requests

Creation Compromise

Key Passages

- Genesis 1–2; Mark 1:14–15; Acts 20:17–21

What You Will Learn

- The basic Christian positions on the creation of the universe and life on earth.
- How the doctrine of creation affects the issues of authority and salvation.

Lesson Overview

As we are confronted with claims about the origin of the universe and the life in it, we must look to Scripture as the first and final authority. Many Christians try to add ideas of long ages and evolutionary thinking to the biblical history of the earth. The church must respond to these issues in a biblical manner.

Memory Verse

Exodus 20:11

For in six days the Lord made the heavens and the earth, the sea, and all that is in them, and rested the seventh day. Therefore the Lord blessed the Sabbath day and hallowed it.

SCRIPTURAL BACKGROUND

Where Scripture speaks clearly on topics, we have no need to explain away those truths—unless some other source becomes our authority. The opening chapters of Genesis speak clearly about the origin of the universe and the method God used to create it. Using the genealogies in Scripture we can conclude the approximate age of the earth. Using the New Testament, we can confirm that Adam and Eve were actual people whom God created.

If we use Scripture as our starting point, and take the Bible as written, we would never come to the conclusion that the universe is billions of years old or that an evolutionary process resulted in life on earth. We would never consider that cancer, death, and diseases—all preserved in the fossil record—were present for billions of years before Adam sinned. We would never consider that Adam and Eve were not actual people or that their creation did not happen as recorded. To come to these conclusions, we must bring ideas into the Bible and ask, "What has God said . . . ?"

Questioning the foundational book of the Bible, especially its opening chapters, allows questions about the rest of the Bible. Questioning the historicity of Adam and Eve directly impacts the believability of the message of the gospel. Paul makes the connection between Adam and the gospel very clear in Romans 5 and 1 Corinthians 15. The salvation that is found in Jesus, the "last Adam," was made necessary because of the sin of the first man, Adam. This doctrine is at the heart of the gospel and is a major challenge facing the church today.

APOLOGETICS BACKGROUND

The attempts to reconcile a world that is believed to be millions or billions of years old have resulted in a variety of views. The following views represent popular views apart from biblical creation. All are attempts to accommodate the interpretation of an earth that is millions or billions of years old.

Gap Theory

Although there are variations, the basic teaching of the gap theory is that millions of years ago God created the universe and everything in it as recorded in Genesis 1:1. Sometime during the subsequent millions of years, Lucifer (i.e., Satan) rebelled and was thrown to earth. This resulted in Lucifer's flood, which destroyed all plant and animal life on earth, thus producing the fossil record in the rock layers.

At the same time as this flood, the earth was plunged into darkness and thus became "without form and void" as recorded in Genesis 1:2. The gap theory teaches that the fossils found in the earth's crust are relics of the originally perfect world that God created, which was supposedly destroyed before the six literal days of creation (or re-creation) recorded in Genesis 1:3–31.

This view was proposed by Thomas Chalmers in the early 1800s to accommodate the scientific ideas of millions of years. It has been popularized by resources such as the Scofield Study Bible. Typically, the age of the earth and universe are left to "science" to determine, but biological evolution is rejected.

Progressive Creation

Progressive Creation is a relatively recent idea that seeks to embrace the big bang as the origin of the universe and to allow for the geological evolution of the earth, but it rejects the biological evolution of life on earth. This view suggests that God created life in spurts and allowed many species to go extinct to be recreated in slightly different forms over billions of years. The days of creation were actually overlapping periods of time during which God created different life forms.

Proponents of this view consider nature to be the "sixty-seventh book of the Bible" and look to that book to teach them about human origins and the history of the earth and universe. The rock layers contain a record of the history of life on earth including pre-humans who did not have a spirit yet strongly resembled humans. The rocks also contain evidence of death, disease, and suffering. The Flood was a local event that is referred to as "universal" because it impacted all humans on the earth at the time.

The view has been popularized by Hugh Ross and the organization Reasons to Believe and is supported by several Christian leaders.

Theistic Evolution

This view is the broadest and includes such diverse ideas that it is hard to define strictly. All theistic evolutionists agree that the secular explanations of the age of the universe and earth are accurate and that the Flood was a local event. All agree that life on earth has evolved from simple organisms. But some believe God created that first spark of life while others believe it happened "naturally" according to the laws God ordained for the universe. Some accept that God had no intervening role in the evolution of life while others see God guiding the process at important steps.

Most agree that humans evolved from previous hominids and God "injected" a spirit into man at some point. Others believe all life was allowed to evolve and at a certain point God specially created Adam and Eve as the first humans. Regardless, the disease, death, and struggle to survive were part of God's original plan for the creation. The days of Genesis 1 are viewed as poetic expressions of the vast ages of earth's history (a day-age interpretation), and there was never a globe-covering Flood.

The day-age view was popularized by Hugh Miller in the early 1800s at the same time Chalmers was espousing the gap theory. As Darwin introduced ideas on biological evolution, those explanations were incorporated into the day-age views and have continued today. Organizations like the Discovery Institute and BioLogos sponsor teachers who teach various forms of theistic evolution.

HISTORICAL BACKGROUND

With few exceptions, Christians until the eighteenth century believed that the earth was young based on the biblical descriptions. It was not until those studying the geology of the earth began to question the age of the earth that these ideas entered the church. Many assume that Darwin was the catalyst for this idea moving into the church, but it happened long before Origin of Species was published.

As a result of the suggestion that the earth is millions of years old from people like Charles Lyell, leaders within the church started to teach those ideas and reinterpret the clear teaching of Scripture. This is when ideas like the gap theory and day-age views began to creep into the church. "Science" was given a position of authority over Scripture with respect to the age of the earth and the days of creation.

While some within the church rejected biological evolution and embraced the idea of long ages of history (Charles Spurgeon would be an example), there were those who stood against the corrupting influences. One group is known as the scriptural geologists, and they used Scripture to combat the old-age interpretation of the rock layers. This battle continues today as the church faces the corrupting influence of adding worldly wisdom to the Word of God. Jesus will build His church, and the wisdom of hell and the world will not prevail against it!

For more information on this topic, see the Online Resource Page.

 Studying God's Word

Can someone believe in evolution and be saved?

Take notes as you study the following passages.

Genesis 1:1–8

Christian Views on Creation

Complete the Christian Views on Creation worksheet.

"What's Wrong with Progressive Creation?" video notes

Take notes as you view the "What's Wrong with Progressive Creation?" video.

Mark 1:14-15

Acts 20:17-21

 God's Word in the Real World

1. If we accept that "scientific" thinking (allowing for
    only natural explanations) is the filter we should use to
    understand the Bible, what other doctrines or events might
    be in danger?

2. How do we decide which of these doctrines or events are so important that we must cling to them as part of orthodox Christianity?

3. One of the key doctrines of Christianity is the sufficiency of Scripture (2 Timothy 3:16; 2 Peter 1:3–4). Many people who hold to the views we have talked about today would say they believe Scripture is sufficient. How would they have to define sufficiency in order to accept theistic evolution or the gap theory?

4. Suppose your child comes to you and asks, "I am hearing that many Christians say God could have used the big bang and evolution to create the universe. Is that something I should believe?" How would you respond?

5. One of the most important questions surrounding the view of the early chapters of Genesis is the question of the origin of death. From a biblical perspective, Adam's sin brought death into God's "very good" creation. How do the various views we have discussed today try and reconcile this problem?

 Prayer Requests

Corruption: Sin Enters the World

Key Passages

- Genesis 3; Revelation 12:9; Hebrews 9:22

What You Will Learn

- The purpose of the first animal death recorded in Scripture.
- God's provision for salvation from sin through the Savior.

Lesson Overview

Sin and death entered the world through Adam. The first death occurred in the garden when God killed an animal to clothe Adam and Eve after they disobeyed Him. This first blood sacrifice pointed to the truth and the reality of the perfect, complete, one-time sacrifice of Jesus Christ for the remission of sins.

Memory Verse

Genesis 2:15–17

Then the Lord God took the man and put him in the garden of Eden to tend and keep it. And the Lord God commanded the man, saying, "Of every tree of the garden you may freely eat; but of the tree of the knowledge of good and evil you shall not eat, for in the day that you eat of it you shall surely die."

Prepare to Learn

SCRIPTURAL BACKGROUND

God created a perfect universe—one that He Himself called very good (Genesis 1:31). So when and how did sin enter the world? Because the creation was perfect, we know there was no sin. We can then conclude that Satan sinned against God and was cast out of heaven sometime after the seventh day of creation and before he tempted Eve. Satan's temptation of Eve marked the point that changed God's perfect creation to a world filled with death, disease, and decay—all a result of sin.

In the account of the temptation and fall into sin from Genesis 3, Satan, more cunning than any beast of the field, challenged the authority of God and deceived Eve into eating the forbidden fruit (Genesis 3:4–5). Adam, who was with her, also ate of the fruit (Genesis 3:6). This first sin was not just the eating of some fruit; it was disobedience toward a holy God.

As they ate, their eyes were opened and they knew they were naked (Genesis 3:7). They felt shame for their nakedness and tried to fashion clothing from leaves to cover their shame. These coverings were not adequate to conceal their sin from God. Nor were they able to hide from Him when He came to the garden (Genesis 3:9). God now had to punish the sin and disobedience of Adam, Eve, and Satan (Genesis 3:14–19). How quickly and easily they fell into the "blame game." Take note that Eve quickly blamed the serpent (Genesis 3:13) and Adam, in turn, blamed Eve. Sadly, Adam ultimately cast the responsibility of his sin onto God (Genesis 3:12).

God's justice requires that He punish any disobedience of His commands, but His mercy allows many to avoid that punishment. The sin that plagues every human entered the world through Adam and was consequently passed to all of his descendants. The doctrine of original sin (demanding God's justice) and redemption (displaying His mercy) is present throughout the Bible and is presented concisely in Romans 5:17–21. It seems unfair that all of us would pay the consequence of one man's sin—but the Bible tells us that our hearts are deceitful and desperately wicked (Jeremiah 17:9). And if we honestly examine our hearts, we know this to be true. Praise God for His immeasurable grace through Jesus Christ (Ephesians 2:7). For it is only by His grace that we can be freed from the wages of our sin—death and eternal punishment (Romans 6:22–23).

Adam and Eve's rebellion did not take God by surprise. God is omniscient—He knows all things. And He did not leave Adam and Eve in despair, but offered them the hope of the promised

Savior—the Seed—who would crush the head of the serpent (Genesis 3:15) and bear the sins of the world on the Cross. This pre-ordained plan for redemption was in place before the foundation of the world and would perfectly exhibit God's mercy to sinners who, through Jesus Christ, believe in God (1 Peter 1:20–21).

APOLOGETICS BACKGROUND

Today many people want to discount the book of Genesis, the account of Adam and Eve, the biblical age of the earth (about 6,000 years old), and the effects of sin on all of mankind. We know that the universe God created during Creation Week was very good (Genesis 1:31). Any very good creation of God's could not include disobedience, death, or suffering, and there were none of these in the garden at Creation. The environment was perfect—even the animals lived peacefully with each other. God had commanded the animals to eat only vegetation (Genesis 1:30).

Adam and Eve were to tend and keep the garden. They were free to enjoy every good gift that God had given them (Genesis 1:28–29). God did prohibit them from eating the fruit of one tree—the tree of the knowledge of good and evil. Eating from this tree would bring death (Genesis 2:16–17).

But, they could not resist the lies of the serpent, and they disobeyed God. They immediately recognized their nakedness, sewed leaves together to cover themselves, and hid from God in shame (Genesis 3:7–8). Their leaves were not sufficient to cover their sins. God had a more appropriate covering—tunics from the skins of animals He must have slain Himself (Genesis 3:21). In this act, the first death is recorded in Scripture. This death provided the coverings for the first sin against God. It was a foreshadowing of the sacrificial system revealed to Moses for the atonement of sin and later the death of Jesus Christ on the Cross for the forgiveness of sins. Scripture tells us that, "without the shedding of blood there is no remission" of sin (Hebrews 9:22). The first blood had been shed—it pointed forward to the blood of the coming Savior.

This glorious account of God's intervention in covering the sins of Adam and Eve gives us solid scriptural grounds to refute evolutionary thinking. Since we understand from Scripture that there was no animal death before sin entered the world, any fossilized remains of dead animals cannot be dated before Adam and Eve. Evolutionary thinking cannot be partnered with a biblical worldview. Anyone who says the rock layers and fossils are billions of years old are accepting death, disease, and suffering before sin when, in fact, they are a consequence of the first sin in the garden (Romans 5:21; 1 Corinthians 15:21–22). Animals could not have been dying millions of years before sin entered the world since, according to God's Word, they started dying after Adam's sin about 6,000 years ago. When we determine to maintain our biblical worldview by the plain reading of Scripture, we can confidently answer the questions the world presents.

HISTORICAL BACKGROUND

Considering the history of sin entering the world, we realize Adam and Eve succumbed to the deceit of Satan shortly after their creation. Although Scripture does not specifically tell us how long Adam and Eve lived in the perfect creation before sinning, we can determine a definite range from a thorough reading of the text. Very little time passed before the Fall. God commanded Adam and Eve to "be fruitful and multiply" (Genesis 1:28) and, because of their perfect bodies, conception would have occurred quickly. But we know that Cain was not conceived until after they were sent from the garden (Genesis 4:1).

So, how many days was it until the Fall? It couldn't have happened on the seventh day of creation since God sanctified and blessed that day (Genesis 2:3). Some commentators suggest it could have been as early as the tenth day. Understanding the sinfulness of our own hearts, this timeframe is not hard to imagine. As we consider the scope of history, virtually all of it has occurred in a cursed universe under the influence of sin. It is all we have ever known, but we have the hope of the new creation to come when the earth will be restored to its original "very good" condition (Revelation 21:4).

For more information on this topic, see the Online Resource Page.

Studying God's Word

How did death come into God's perfect creation?

Take notes as you study the following passages.

Genesis 3:1–7

Revelation 12:9

Genesis 3:8–25

Hebrews 9:22

 ## The Plan

In Genesis 3:15 we see the first glimpse of a remedy for the sin that Adam and Eve brought into the world. God promised to send a Seed that will bruise the head of the serpent. This is often referred to as the *protoevangelium* as it is the first hint of the gospel—God would send a Savior through Eve's descendants.

Read the following passages and identify when this plan to send a Savior was put into place. Next to each passage, write the phrase that gives the timeframe of the origin of God's plan to redeem a people for Himself.

1 Peter 1:20–21

Acts 2:22–24

Ephesians 1:3–6

Revelation 13:8

Did God react to the sin and come up with a plan to remedy the situation?

What comfort do you find in knowing that God has a full knowledge of the future?

God's Word in the Real World

1. How is the question that Satan asked Eve in Genesis 3:1 still found in our world today?

2. Many people, even some who claim to be Christians, will make the claim that God did not know Adam and Eve would sin when He created them. How could you use the Bible to demonstrate the flaw in their thinking?

3. If you were discussing the gospel with someone and they said that God was too harsh in cursing Adam and Eve for eating a piece of fruit, how would you respond to help them understand the gravity of the situation?

4. Like Adam and Eve tried to cover their sin by sewing leaves together, in what ways do we try to cover our own sins today, even though we know Christ has already paid for them?

Prayer Requests

10
Effects of the Fall

Key Passages

- Genesis 1:29–31; Deuteronomy 32:4; Genesis 3:14–19; Romans 8:19–22; Revelation 21:1–5

What You Will Learn

- The extent of the effects of the Curse.
- The effects of the Fall that will be reversed in the Consummation.

Lesson Overview

The effects of Adam's Fall have impacted everything in the creation. From the death that would come to Adam—and every person—to the death of animals beginning with those that were used to cover Adam and Eve's sin, the entire creation is now groaning under the effects of sin.

Memory Verse

Genesis 2:15–17

Then the Lord God took the man and put him in the garden of Eden to tend and keep it. And the Lord God commanded the man, saying, "Of every tree of the garden you may freely eat; but of the tree of the knowledge of good and evil you shall not eat, for in the day that you eat of it you shall surely die."

SCRIPTURAL BACKGROUND

What was life like before the Fall of man? Can we even imagine it? Probably not. However, there are some clues in Scripture that help us understand a bit of life in a perfect world.

First of all, there was no death. Death came as a result of Adam's sin (Romans 5:12), and is called an enemy that God will one day destroy (1 Corinthians 15:25–26). Secondly, the earth that God created was "very good" (Genesis 1:31; Deuteronomy 32:4). There were no hurricanes, tsunamis, earthquakes, or other destructive events. God upheld His creation perfectly. Thirdly, man and the animals were vegetarian (Genesis 1:29–30). There were no animals eating other animals, and Adam and Eve did not eat meat. In fact, permission to eat meat did not come until after the Genesis Flood (Genesis 9:1–3). And finally, Adam and Eve had a perfect relationship with their Creator. He spoke with them and they experienced unbroken fellowship with God.

The day that Adam and Eve disobeyed their Creator has been called the saddest day in the history of the universe. God had given them a perfect creation—no death, disease, or suffering. They had been given dominion over the animals, and were told to be fruitful and multiply (Genesis 1:28). However, Eve was tempted by the serpent (Satan) and she ate the fruit that God had forbidden them to eat. Adam joined her in her rebellion, and the world has never been the same.

As a result of their rebellion, God punished the serpent (Genesis 3:14), the woman (Genesis 3:16), and the man (Genesis 3:17). The serpent was cursed more than all the beasts; he would crawl on his belly, and eat dust. And, in a spiritual sense, one day Satan's head would be crushed by the seed of the woman—Jesus (Genesis 3:15)! The woman was subjected to increased pain in childbirth, and the desire to rule over her husband (Genesis 3:16). The ground was cursed on account of the man; it would now bring forth thorns and thistles, and with difficulty man would eat of its fruit (Genesis 3:17–18). Man would now die: "In the sweat of your face you shall eat bread till you return to the ground, for out of it you were taken; for dust you are, and to dust you shall return" (Genesis 3:19).

The Fall and the subsequent Curse brought disaster to the very good creation. We are now experiencing the futility, the groans, and the pains of a universe subject to darkness because of sin (Romans 8:19–20).

We are all affected by the Fall—not only by the Curse God placed on the universe but also by sin. Because every human is a descendant of Adam and Eve, we are born with the same sin nature found in Adam (Romans 3:23). Consequently, we are all bound by the Curse and must endure the distress, pain, suffering, disease, and natural disasters that accompany it. But that is not the end of the story. For we know that Jesus Christ, our Redeemer, has overcome death (1 Corinthians 15:54–55). And all who repent of their sins and turn to Jesus Christ alone for forgiveness will be redeemed to enjoy eternity in the perfectly restored universe—a universe that promises the end of death, sorrow, crying, and pain (Revelation 21:4). We eagerly await this with hope and expectation of finally seeing our Savior face to face (Job 19:26–27).

APOLOGETICS BACKGROUND

The account of the Fall often presents controversy. One of the issues discussed involves animals. If everything was perfectly peaceful in the garden, as Genesis 1 and 2 indicate, then why are so many animals designed with features and structures that seem suited for attacking, tearing, killing, and eating? Scripture tells us that animals were originally vegetarian (Genesis 1:29–30). So, how did they acquire their ability to kill? Where did these defense/attack structures come from?

Creationists have suggested several answers that make sense and fit within the biblical text:

- Originally, these features had a good purpose, but as the environment changed, the purpose for these features had to change as well.

- God added new features to creatures at the Curse so they would be able to withstand the onslaught of violence provoked by sin.

- Although not necessary in a perfect world, God designed the original creatures with the features they would need to live in the fallen world God knew was coming.

- God placed designs for these features in the genes of the original creatures, but they did not become active until after the Curse.

While we do not know exactly how the animals acquired these defense/attack structures, this we do know: according to God's Word, our final authority, animals will once again get along with each other and with man (Isaiah 11:6–7).

HISTORICAL BACKGROUND

The history of the Bible can be divided into three great periods: the pre-Fall world, the post-Fall world, and the Consummation.

The pre-Fall world: God's original creation was perfect—no sin, no disease, no death, and perfect relationships with one another and the Creator. Because of our present sin-cursed world, riddled with decay and death, it is hard to even imagine the pre-Fall world!

The post-Fall world: The Fall of man and subsequent Curse of Genesis 3 affected the entire creation. This is why the Apostle Paul describes our present world as "groaning together in the pains of childbirth until now" (Romans 8:22). The creation is broken; it is in "bondage to corruption" (Romans 8:21). Sin, disease, carnivory, natural disasters, and death are the course of this present world—"red in tooth and claw" as Tennyson wrote. The sin in the Garden of Eden affected the whole cosmos.

The Consummation: At the Consummation, when Christ shall return as Judge and King, the Curse will be removed. God will sum up all things in Christ, putting all enemies under His feet, and death itself will be destroyed. The new heaven and new earth will be a return to Eden-like agricultural fruitfulness (Ezekiel 47:12; Revelation 22:1–3), and perfect harmony in human relationships (1 Corinthians 13:8–12), in animal life (Isaiah 11:6–8), and in everything under the rule of the Son of Man, the Lord Jesus. Earth will receive her King, and all will be restored. What a glorious hope we have!

For more information on this topic, see the Online Resource Page.

Studying God's Word

How much of God's creation was affected by the Fall?

A Cursed Creation

Because God is just, He must punish sin. This was the case with the first human sin, and we see the description of God's judgment on that sin in Genesis 3.

Carefully read through Genesis 3:8–19. Remember to keep the context in mind. Organize the information about the curses pronounced by God in a chart or list in the space below. Give as much detail as you can.

"Was there Death Before Adam Sinned?" video notes

Take notes as you view the "Was There Death Before Adam Sinned?" video.

Take notes as you study the following passages.

Genesis 1:29-31

Deuteronomy 32:4

Genesis 9:1-3

Romans 8:19-22

Revelation 21:1-5

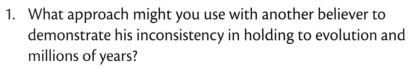
God's Word in the Real World

1. What approach might you use with another believer to demonstrate his inconsistency in holding to evolution and millions of years?

2. What assurance do you find in thinking about the future Consummation knowing that the original creation of God was perfect and included no death or suffering?

3. How might your view be different if you believed the original state of God's creation included animals eating each other to survive?

4. How can an understanding of the nature and extent of the Fall help you understand the evil that exists in the world?

5. How can understanding the Fall help you find comfort when you face a situation like cancer, the death of a child, or the chaos of a tornado striking your town?

 Prayer Requests

11

Cain and Abel

Key Passages

- Genesis 4:1–17; Hebrews 11:4;
  1 John 3:10–12; Genesis 3:20, 5:4

What You Will Learn

- How Cain's offering differed from Abel's offering.
- How God's mercy and justice shown to Cain relates to the gospel.

Lesson Overview

The sacrifices of Cain and Abel reveal God's demand for a pure heart of worship toward Him. The first human death occurred when Cain murdered Abel out of jealousy. In this account God reveals that He is just to punish sin yet merciful to sinners as well.

Memory Verse

Genesis 2:15–17

Then the Lord God took the man and put him in the garden of Eden to tend and keep it. And the Lord God commanded the man, saying, "Of every tree of the garden you may freely eat; but of the tree of the knowledge of good and evil you shall not eat, for in the day that you eat of it you shall surely die."

📖 Prepare to Learn

SCRIPTURAL BACKGROUND

The sin committed at the Fall of man through the disobedience of Adam and Eve in the garden (Genesis 3:6–7) brought corruption on the human race. Adam and Eve were cursed by God (Genesis 3:16–17) and sent out of the garden (Genesis 3:24). Eve had two sons—Cain and Abel. As they grew, Abel was a keeper of the sheep, but Cain tilled the ground (Genesis 4:1–2). After some time, they each brought an offering to the Lord—Cain some of the "fruit of the ground," and Abel "the first-born of his flock" (Genesis 4:3–4). In Genesis we are simply told that "the Lord respected Abel and his offering, He did not respect Cain and his offering" (4:4–5). But why?

Various Scriptures from the New Testament help to solve this puzzle. The book of Hebrews records that Abel made his offering "by faith" and that "he was righteous" (Hebrews 11:4). Cain, however, was of the wicked one and murdered his brother because his works were evil (1 John 3:11–12).

Cain's actions spoke loudly of the desires of his heart. Because of his jealousy, he killed his brother—who walked by faith in righteousness toward God.

And God used this unlikely scenario to display His gracious mercy. God is a holy God and, because of His holiness, had to judge Cain's sin. But instead of requiring a life for a life as the law demanded (Exodus 21:23–24), God spared Cain, making him a fugitive and vagabond on the earth—a fugitive specially marked by God and protected from those seeking revenge for his offense (Genesis 4:14–15).

The effects of the Fall came fast and furious. It doesn't take long for sin to corrupt and this first murder illustrates that. In the first generation after Adam and Eve, we see jealousy, selfishness, and hatred. And yet, God was already revealing the depths of the mercy in His character—a mercy that has repeatedly been demonstrated as man continues to disobey God in his sinfulness.

APOLOGETICS BACKGROUND

"Then Cain went out from the presence of the Lord and dwelt in the land of Nod on the east of Eden. And Cain knew his wife" (Genesis 4:16–17).

One of the most-asked questions about the book of Genesis is, "Where did Cain get his wife?" This question is often used by skeptics to discredit the historical truth of the book of Genesis because most Christians don't know how to answer it. If Adam and Eve were the first humans, and if their first two sons were Cain and Abel, then where did Mrs. Cain come from? Some have answered this by saying that God must have created other people or races on earth who did not descend from Adam and Eve. However, Scripture is very clear that ALL people are descendants of Eve (Genesis 3:20). And since only descendants of Adam and Eve can be saved, believers need to be able to show that Cain's wife—like all other humans—was a descendant of Adam and Eve.

The answer to this question is, in fact, quite simple: Cain married his sister or perhaps another close relative like a niece. Genesis 5:3–4 states:

> And Adam lived one hundred and thirty years, and begot a son in his own likeness, after his image, and named him Seth. After he begot Seth, the days of Adam were eight hundred years; and he had sons and daughters.

Notice that after Seth was born (Adam's third son), Adam and Eve had "sons and daughters." Exactly how many, we aren't told, but given that Adam lived more than 900 years, it could have been a lot! One Jewish tradition states that Adam had 33 sons and 23 daughters.

Many people reject this very clear answer, citing the law against brother-sister marriages. But keep in mind that way back then (about 6,000 years ago) close relatives could marry—they had to in order to start their own families. Even Abraham married his half-sister (Genesis 20:12).

It was not until much later—2,500 years after Cain married his wife—that God commanded Moses that people were not to marry close relatives (Leviticus 18:6). We know now that this command, directed by the providence of God, protects us from many genetic deformities that could result from the marrying of close relatives. These deformities are one of the results of sin and its consequences, which brought disease and death to God's perfect creation. God's Word gives us answers. We need to approach all questions with biblical glasses, standing on the authority of the Scripture—knowing that the Bible is our starting point.

HISTORICAL BACKGROUND

In the account of Cain and Abel, we see that God respected the offering of Abel (Genesis 4:4). Abel's offering was the firstborn of his flock—an animal offering presented with a pure heart. As we look at animal offerings throughout biblical history, we can see the amazing foreshadowing and significance of them.

The very first animal sacrifice was made by God Himself to cover the nakedness of Adam and Eve after they had disobeyed and introduced sin to the human race (Genesis 3:20–21). Adam and Eve deserved instant death because of their sin, yet we see God displaying His glorious mercy as He killed the animal(s) to make garments as coverings for the sinners.

In hindsight we can see how this is a foreshadowing of the substitutionary death of an animal to pay for sin. The foundational elements of God's plan of redemption are shown here on the occasion of the first sin in the Garden of Eden.

Scripture tells us of more customary animal sacrifices ordained by God. Noah sacrificed animals after the Flood (Genesis 8:20), Job sacrificed animals for the sins of his family (Job 1:5), and Abraham sacrificed the ram that God provided as a substitute for Isaac (Genesis 22:13). Clearly, God had revealed the concept of substitutionary sacrifice long before the time of Moses and the Law.

However, it was at the time of Moses, when the Israelites left Egypt, that God specifically appointed a sacrificial system to cover the sins of His people. Leviticus 17:11 states "For the life of the flesh is in the blood, and I have given it to you upon the altar to make atonement for your souls; for it is the blood that makes atonement for the soul." In this system, the life of the animal atoned for—or covered—the offenses of the sinner; the animal died as a substitute for the sinner.

We know, of course, that animal sacrifices can never cleanse us from our sin. Scripture states, ". . . in those [Old Testament] sacrifices there is a reminder of sins every year. For it is not possible that the blood of bulls and goats could take away sins" (Hebrews 10:3–4). The ultimate purpose of the sacrificial system was to demonstrate that the penalty for sin is death (Romans 6:23). It was God's way of preparing us to receive and believe in the perfect Lamb of God whose blood would finally take away the sins of all who would turn to Him in repentance and faith (John 1:29).

This we know, that before the universe was created, before time existed, before man was formed, God knew that we (in Adam) would sin. He also had a predetermined plan by which salvation for our sins could be received through the free gift of grace by the death of the perfect sacrifice—Jesus Christ, the sinless Son of God and only Savior.

What an amazing God we serve! "For the Lord is good; His mercy is everlasting, and His truth endures to all generations" (Psalm 100:5).

For more information on this topic, see the Online Resource Page.

Studying God's Word

Why was Cain's sacrifice rejected?

Take notes as you study the following passages.

Genesis 4:1–15

An Acceptable Sacrifice

Complete the An Acceptable Sacrifice worksheet.

Genesis 4:16–17

Genesis 3:20

Genesis 5:4

_____

_____

_____

_____

 ## God's Word in the Real World

1. How can we relate the things that we do to please God (our offerings) to the offerings Cain and Abel presented?

2. Hebrews 13:15–16 calls us to "offer the sacrifice of praise to God" not forgetting "to do good and to share" as God is pleased with such sacrifices. How is this apparent in the account of Cain and Abel and in your life?

3. How does sin's pattern found in James 1:13–15 compare to what we see in the account of Cain, and how can that help us understand why we sin and how to avoid it?

4. Abel offered the firstborn of his flock, and elsewhere we see the idea of God honoring the firstfruits offered to him. How can we apply this idea to our offerings to God today?

5. How can you relate the mercy shown to Cain to the mercy shown to you through Christ?

Prayer Requests

12
The Hearts of Man

Key Passages

- Romans 3:23, 5:12–21; Genesis 6:5, 8:21;
  Psalm 51:5; Jeremiah 17:9; John 3:16–21;
  1 Corinthians 15:21–22

What You Will Learn

- That all men are sinners through the sin
  of Adam.

- That Jesus Christ paid the penalty for
  our sins.

Lesson Overview

Since the very first sin of Adam in the garden, all people are born into sin. We inherited this sin nature from Adam, whom God accounted as the representative of the human race. Our sin deserves death and eternal separation from God. But in His grace and mercy God has provided forgiveness through Jesus Christ—the perfect sacrifice.

Memory Verse

Genesis 2:15–17

Then the Lord God took the man and put him in the garden of Eden to tend and keep it. And the Lord God commanded the man, saying, "Of every tree of the garden you may freely eat; but of the tree of the knowledge of good and evil you shall not eat, for in the day that you eat of it you shall surely die."

SCRIPTURAL BACKGROUND

We saw the effects of sin begin to ravage the world and its culture in the children of Adam and Eve. The first murder occurred when Cain killed his brother Abel out of greed, jealousy, selfishness, and hatred. The Bible tells us that evil company corrupts good habits (1 Corinthians 15:33), and it appears Cain was quick to influence those around him with the evil in his heart.

The Bible tells us of Lamech—the fifth generation from Cain. His heart was corrupted and we know that he took two wives (Genesis 4:19) in rebellion to God's ordinance of marriage (Genesis 2:24). We read how he speaks with seeming pride of another murder—this one he committed (Genesis 4:23). As the moral fiber decayed from generation to generation we can only imagine what the Lord saw as He looked upon the earth. For He was grieved in His heart that He had made people and knew that He must destroy them (Genesis 6:5–7).

And what does the Lord see today? More sin, evil, and corruption. Since Adam and Eve disobeyed God and were sent from the garden, their sin nature has been passed on to all humans. The Bible states that death spread to all men through the sin of Adam (Romans 5:12). In Adam all die—because of sin. But in Christ all shall be made alive (1 Corinthians 15:22).

As descendants of Adam and Eve, we have all inherited a sin nature. David knew that he was conceived in sin—an inheritance from Adam (Psalm 51:5). And Jeremiah reminds us that the heart is deceitful above all things and desperately wicked (Jeremiah 17:9). Our sin demands judgment by a holy God. Jesus tells us that judgment is coming. Speaking of the final judgment, He warns that just like it was in the days of Noah, so it will be also in the days of the Son of Man (Luke 17:26). He is coming to judge the world with righteousness and the peoples with His truth (Psalm 96:13).

So what are we to do? We know that our God—our holy, jealous God—is a consuming fire who will not tolerate our loyalty, love, honor, and respect being placed anywhere else (Deuteronomy 4:23–24). He is intolerant of sin, and we are all sinners (Romans 3:23).

"But thanks be to God, who gives us the victory through our Lord Jesus Christ" (1 Corinthians 15:57). For God had always known that He would send "His only begotten Son, that whoever believes in Him should not perish but have everlasting life" (John 3:16). Through Him alone are we brought from darkness into light and from the power of Satan to God. Through Jesus our Savior we receive forgiveness of our sins and the inheritance of eternity with Him (Acts 26:18).

APOLOGETICS BACKGROUND

Man has always suffered from a self-centered arrogance that bristles at the very thought of being sinful at heart. Many truly believe that humans are inherently good and that it is unthinkable that we are born into sin. Couple this thinking with the self-esteem rhetoric that maintains we are great—we better know it, believe it, and be very impressed by it. We can see that we are raising a generation that can't fathom they are deceitful and wicked—that their hearts desire only to rebel against God (Jeremiah 17:9).

We tell our children to follow their hearts. Whatever they imagine they can do, they can. Their dreams are theirs if they only wish for them. Whatever they feel in their heart is OK, and they must pursue their heart's desire. However, this is not what God's Word tells us. We are leading our children astray with this type of teaching. Our feelings cannot lead our decisions. Our hearts are fickle and wicked. Our lives should be directed by Scripture alone. The Word of God will direct us in all righteousness. The righteousness of His testimonies is everlasting—with understanding in these, we shall live (Psalm 119:144).

Without a proper understanding of the depth of the sin in our hearts, how can we properly rejoice at the forgiveness that is ours through Christ? If our sin is minor or inconsequential in our eyes, what would make us turn from it and accept the free gift of forgiveness and salvation from God? If we long for the pleasures of our heart and pursue those desires without considering God's Word, how would we make Him the Lord and King of our lives? With our own needs and comforts so much in view, how would we ever be able to properly humble ourselves before God to plead His mercy and forgiveness? Do you see? The very gospel is at stake when we consider the self-esteem-building philosophy so many are buying into.

The Apostle Paul sums it up well this way: "For I know that in me (that is, in my flesh) nothing good dwells" (Romans 7:18). We are sinners. Our righteousness is like filthy rags before the Lord (Isaiah 64:6). And it is only through humble repentance and belief in the gospel of Jesus Christ (Mark 1:15) that we will escape the judgment and condemnation for our sins.

But the good news is that God promises a new heart for those who trust in Christ and thereby become partakers of the New Covenant (Jeremiah 31:33–34; Hebrews 8:6–12). We become new creations in Christ (2

Corinthians 5:17), and can walk in newness of life, no longer living as slaves to sin (Romans 6:1–7).

HISTORICAL BACKGROUND

It wasn't long after creation that sin entered the world. Adam and Eve coveted what they could not have and in direct disobedience to God went after it. God's judgment came upon them in the form of a curse, and they were expelled from the garden (Genesis 3:24). Their fellowship with God was broken. Now sin would be a part of the human race.

We know that "those who are in the flesh cannot please God" (Romans 8:8) and that in our sin we are lawless, insubordinate, ungodly, unholy, profane, murderers, manslayers, fornicators, sodomites, kidnappers, liars, and perjurers (1 Timothy 1:9–10). With this in mind, it is not surprising that, just 1,600 years after Adam and Eve were sent from the presence of God, He once again had to judge the sin of the world. This time it was a worldwide Flood that would destroy all but Noah and his family (Genesis 6:13, 6:18). Sin continued to pervade the lives of the people.

It was just more than 100 years after God destroyed the world that His judgment fell at Babel. The people were disobedient to God's direct commands and desired to build themselves a city and a tower to the heavens. They longed to make a great name for themselves (Genesis 11:4). These plans angered the holy God and He judged them by confusing their language and scattering the people across the face of all the earth (Genesis 11:7–8).

And man continues to sin. God is now withholding His full judgment on the unjust—but it will come (2 Peter 2:9–11). He is coming to judge the earth in righteousness (Psalm 98:9). His judgment is real and eternal, and will come by fire. "But the heavens and the earth which are now preserved by the same word, are reserved for fire until the day of judgment and perdition of ungodly men" (2 Peter 3:7). But thanks be to God that we can escape God's wrath and judgment through faith in Christ (Romans 5:9; 1 Thessalonians 5:9).

For more information on this topic, see the Online Resource Page.

Studying God's Word

Is it wise to follow your heart?

Take notes as you study the following passages.

Romans 5:12–21

Romans 3:23

Genesis 6:5

Genesis 8:21

Psalm 51:5

Jeremiah 17:9

Pop Culture vs. Scripture

Complete the Pop Culture vs. Scripture worksheet.

John 3:16–21

1 Corinthians 15:21–22

_____

_____

_____

 ## God's Word in the Real World

1. What evidence could you offer to someone who doubts that all people are sinful from conception?

2. If you believe that the doctrine of original sin is unfair, would it be consistent to look for salvation from your sin through the sacrifice of Jesus on the Cross?

3. If sin is passed to all of Adam's descendants, why is it important to affirm that Adam and Eve were the original parents of all people?

4. What hope do you find in knowing that you can look to what Christ has done for assurance of your salvation rather than looking to your own works to commend you to God?

5. How has this lesson helped you understand the need to share the gospel with those around you?

Prayer Requests